REBEAT

BECAUSE
THE BEAT MUST POUND

BY S. E. MCKENZIE

DEDICATION
To everyone who has been left out in the cold

THIS BOOK IS A BOOK OF SPECULATIVE FICTION
Characters, companies, governments, places, events, are either
products of the author's imagination or used fictitiously. Any
resemblance to persons (living or dead), companies, governments,
places and/or events, is a coincidence and unintended.

TABLE OF CONTENTS

ReBeat
I

ReBeat; goes my heart;
Repeat; we tear each other apart;
Defeat; only one can win

At Sum Zero game play.

Tic Toc
Goes my clock;
Time does not knock

But only barges in to create a shock;
Impure Fusion needs Fission;
Still a hard decision

For there is an ocean
Inside me; attracts; reacts;
Pulls me back and forth with my inner tides;

Splitting; competing
Towards Sum Zero.
No one needs to be a hero;

Dodging time's touch;
Just another
Sum Zero game to play;

Blame the loser for losing;
Praise the winner for winning.
Logical; philosophical;

Sum Zero game play;
So practical
For those living in the Ivory Tower

Over there;
Why should they care
About here?

While we all had
Our eyes closed
In prayer; surrounded by Fear.

Pete buried what was left of his past;
Could no longer climb
The steep steps fast;

ReBeat

Leading to the top of the Ivory Tower;
"Do you really have to ask
If Hate is older than Love?"

I heard him scream;
Awoken from his broken dream.
"Do you really care?

You, so protected up there."

Then I knew, what old man Pete
Must have been going through;
Now, I could feel his tear drops

Accumulating around my feet.
Old man Pete;
Always acting as if he were elite;

Today, he faced defeat.

Hate so toxic filled the air;
Strategically placed
In every war and everywhere.

Sending us back to zero
With nowhere else
To go.

Few would dare to care.
While Hate was consuming Goodwill
Just to irritate Fate;

Made Love come too late;
As Hate initiated even more Hate;
So much more than ever before.

Destroying Harmony
While Fear and Despair
Crushed Talent before it could grow;

From today into tomorrow
All that was left was sorrow;
If it had not been for the Hope

We had to borrow.

Many were hanging
By Gestapo's rope
Fooled by Gestapo's dope.

ReBeat

II

Everyone is waiting for a miracle;
But all I see
Is how they crushed

The Tree
Of Unity.
Now, how will we ever be free?

Stakeholder;
Life blood
Of every entity;

Spilled all over the ground;
The shock
Made my heart pound;

Too many Souls to count;
Hanging
From the Tree of Unity;

By Gestapo's rope;

They were fooled
By Gestapo's dope
And are now no more;

No longer able to touch
All the things
That they used to love so much;

Ghosts flying into the atmosphere;
Up above and not so clear
Sort of free from all this fear.

And Gestapo
Never had to shed a tear
The bodies were not even near;

He was the ruler; that never had to lead;

He was the fooler inspired by greed;
Ignoring all the underfed that he refused to feed;
That were overkilled

In all this greed.

ReBeat

Sum Zero game was his only strategy;
Never meant to prevent a tragedy;
Just a mindless travesty;

Escalating as World War Three;

War Machinery
Without a heart;
ReBeat cannot start;

Repeat; History
One more time
Again.

As Pete refused defeat;
He climbed the steps
Hidden inside

The Ivory Tower;
Soon he could see
So much more;

If only they would have opened the door.

Toxic Town so divided and torn apart;
Everyone wants control
So they micro-manage their Soul;

Freezing motion in time;
Confusion
While impure Fusion needs Fission to start.

Avoid relating
To the unknown
Unkempt generation;

So Frozen in time
All they could do was shiver and linger;
Trapped inside their two faced world

They could not guard their back
As they played
The Sum Zero game.

Defeat; no one can win;
As they all forgot to feed the beast
That now must hunt;

ReBeat

Too complicated
For Bureaucracy
To stop.

Old man Pete;
Black hair dye; not much to eat;
Grumbles as he stumbles in the Ivory Tower.

Old man Pete
Cannot defy
The Force of Time.

Never walking lightly;
Absentee landlords
Roll in their dough

From Micro Plots
Packed and stacked
From the ceiling to the floor;

All on top of each other;
Not much room for more;
Nowhere else to go.

The ones so moneyed;
Had only one motivator
And it was their greed;

Leaving nothing for their brother.
In the wasted land;
So many left behind;

Looking for a way to feed
All of those
Breaking down in need.

Even though spring
Was in the air
Cruelty was called fair;

For it was everywhere.

As the flood gates opened their doors;
The Gong Show began.
In Backward Nation

Can only predict the past;
Always afraid
Of being last;

ReBeat

The King of Bling
Stands at his
Bully Pulpit

While impure Fusion
Needs Fission
To start.

Perfect Platform
To project
His Holy Agenda;

To us; Just another secret;
Everyone wants
Power; so they take it from others;

To win
The Sum Zero
Game.

So willing to let another
Lose the most
In order to win the most;

"I will blame a Holy Ghost.
When this Sum Zero game
Hurts you the most,"

Said the crying child;
Lost in a loop
Of destroyed morale;

Has no one else to cling to
But
The King of Bling.

Polarized;
Stigmatized;
Too easy to lose;

For people on same side;
Sum Zero Game;
Is close to suicide;

Too easy to play.

ReBeat

If it were not for God watching;
And the hope for a ride to Heaven
And everlasting Life;

Where the dead poets live after life;
Many dying by their own hands;
Grew weaker than their words

Which imprisoned their minds;

Hate; toxic mind control;
Between the haves and have nots;
And those that spin the loop;

Some get lost inside their minds;
Others get lost in the Wasted Land;
While Nouveau Gestapo

Stomps out the Beat.
So many
Are too willing to repeat.

While spinning the loop.
To stay positive
In the Wasted Land

S.E. McKENZIE

That stopped believing in love
A long time ago;
When life's beat was slow

But hard;
Rhythmic interaction
In the Wasted Land;

Many followed the God of Love;
Not yet captured
By the God of War;

So able to rule;
But could not lead;
For there would have been too many

For him to feed.

While the Wasted Land fell;
Burned
Like Hell.

Two sides
To everything
Or so it seems

ReBeat

As water flows out
Into streams
That will never be free

For the water is trapped in currents
Controlled by the pull
Of the sun and moon.

Hear the screams;
Everything is now gone
That they worked for;

The control freaks laugh out loud
For they have won
The game of Sum Zero;

The circle must now be respun
For it can never be undone
Without losing a life.

A life worth fighting for;
Now we too
Believe in War.

Just the way so many have done before;
For we want the beat
To go on for evermore;

To never stop;
For life as we know it
Will then stop too.

III

Wasted Land under a new command;
Depopulation
Began when they brought in strangers

From a distant land
Who began to kill
All those who could no longer

Pay their bill;

The locals screamed out in pain
As they realized
That they were betrayed

ReBeat

One more time again,

For public property was never free;
Now privately
Micro-managed

By the power clique;
Blurring civil with criminal;
Blurring an assumption with a lie;

Blurring suicide
With fatal error;
Class distinction

No more.

Without a face
Or a place
To call one's own;

Even the dead had nowhere to go;
They roamed
Unable to touch

Everything that they had loved so much.

IV

Noble Man;
Just a man of fiction;
No longer shocked were we

To find the real man not noble at all;
Gaining his advantage
Through exploiting fear of others;

Even his sisters and brothers;

So much fear was flowing
And showing
Surrounding the Lost

Who were hiding in the Wasted Land;
Descendants of the enemy
Who changed sides;

A long time ago.

His Negative Bias was beginning to show;
Burnt the only bridge found
Now we have to walk around

ReBeat

The current
Which is violent at times;
Could pull us all in.

V

Fusion
The power of the sun and stars;
Reaction to two hydrogen atoms

Combined
Could blow my mind;
Distance

Is what keeps me safe;
Only for a moment;
Until my life is crushed

By the Sum Zero game;
Then I must
Start all over again.

VI

Fission
Escaping neutrons
Strike

Terror in all they surround;
Melting the ground;
Consuming itself.

Fission to set off impure Fusion;
Process to fit into a missile;
But all I see is a tool for a fool

Lost in delusion;

Who can only rule;
But never lead;
Turning away;

With nothing good to say;
Closing his eyes
As his people starve.

THE END

Produced by S.E. McKenzie Productions
First Print Edition December 2015

Enquiries: 1(778)992-2453
Mailing Address:
S. E. McKenzie Productions
168 B 5ᵗʰ St.
Courtenay, BC
V9N 1J4

Email Address:
messidartha@aol.com

http://www.amazon.com/SarahMcKenzie/e/B00H9RWX48/

www.ingramcontent.com/pod-product-compliance
Lightning Source LLC
Chambersburg PA
CBHW060549030426
42337CB00021B/4505